# Writing Well

## (for the rest of us)

No Grammar. No Rules.
Just Common Sense.

Alex Eckelberry

PUBLISHED BY ST. THOMAS PRESS

Published in the United States by St. Thomas Press, Tampa, Florida.

"For the Rest of Us" is a trademark of Technology Growth Engineering.
Graphic attribution: Renee Ramsey-Passmore.

ISBN-13: 978-1505528374
ISBN-10: 1505528372

Eckelberry, Alexander (2015-3-7). Writing Well (for the rest of us): No
Grammar. Nor Rules. Just Common Sense. St. Thomas Press.

# Contents

# Read this first.

This book is written for the average English writer who has difficulty knowing how to write well. It can also be used by students in middle or high school, or for those studying English as a Second Language. That's why the language in this book is very, very simple.

It is not designed for people who already know how to write well, or for those who already have a solid understanding of the rules of grammar. They might get a book such as *The Elements of Style* (along with the excellent companion, *On Writing Well*).

The problem people face these days is that they can get anything they want off the internet, but most reference sources are often too complicated for the average person.

So, I have used simple language throughout this book, with the hope that it is useful to the broadest audience possible. I've specifically made things less complicated, and this *does* mean that I have skipped over some things that people highly educated in grammar will howl over. Well, this is not written for highly educated people. If you are highly educated in grammar, you don't need this book.

(If you're adventurous, there is a section at the end of the book where I get into more detail, but I don't want to lose you along the way with anything complicated.)

I wrote this book because modern-day writing has become terrible. I see many errors in all forms of writing, from simple emails to school papers.

In an online world, you write all the time and are judged by how well you write. You may post a message on Facebook, send a message on a dating site, use email, or write a blog. You don't want to look poorly educated.

One can suppose that good writing has been lost for a number of reasons. I won't speculate as to why, although I suspect it has a lot to do with the generally poor state of education these days.

Unfortunately, I can't teach you *how* to become a great writer. The best way to learn to write well is to read well-written books (or even magazines and online articles), write a lot, and ask for help when you need it.

I can, however, help you with tips that I learned along the way myself, from stern-faced English teachers, fellow writers, and a lot of study. I love this language, and I've spent my life learning about it.

Am I a great writer? Not really. I'm decent, and I still make mistakes myself. I've done something, however, that not many people get a chance to do: While I am a professional CEO, I've spent a great part of my career doing professional writing. I started my career as a technical and marketing writer and later, became a fairly well-known writer in the online world. One thing I learned early on was to have no shame. I would take anything I had written to the smartest writer I knew and ask him or her to tear it to pieces. I learned a lot that way. Practice makes (nearly) perfect.

I hope this books helps you to become a better writer. However, I know that my work is not complete and I'm always looking for feedback. Email me from my website (www.becomeabetterwriter.org) and let me know your thoughts, or where you could use some help. I consider this book a "living document" and will continue to update it from time to time.

# Think Different.

Steve Jobs, the leader of Apple Computer, created moans and groans from English teachers across the world when he came up with the marketing slogan "think different."

To some, it's a grammatical catastrophe.

However, most people don't even know *why* the grammar might be wrong (and it may not be wrong, if you believe Steve Jobs' explanation, which I cover much later in this book).

Jobs was no fool – he was fairly well educated and knew his grammar. He was just trying to get your attention (and it worked).

The point is not whether or not he did a bad thing. The point is that you should know yourself when the grammar is bad, and if you're going to make mistakes, at least do them *knowing* you're making a mistake.

### The problem: People hate grammar

You say "grammar" to someone and they want to run for the hills, because grammar is generally taught so poorly. It's full of complicated rules that often don't make much sense. (In the United States, it's not even "grammar" anymore – it's often part of a hodgepodge subject called "Language Arts." I still don't understand what that term means.)

But what is grammar? The word itself comes from the Greek *graphein,* meaning "to draw or write." It's the rules of writing and speaking.

Grammar should not be intended to make you feel stupid, or to allow someone else to feel smarter than you.

You must write well to do well in this world, whether you're selling, waiting tables or mowing lawns. If you're selling, you'd better have a good grasp of the language; if you're waiting tables, you need to write so that the cook understands the food order; if you're mowing lawns, you need to be able to send an understandable invoice to your customers so you get paid.

Imagine this: You're playing a sport and you keep breaking the rules. People will get upset with you. The same goes for the rules of grammar. People who know the rules will get upset, even just a little bit.

## But do you need to know grammar?

You need to know *a bit* of grammar, but there's a lot of information you don't need to get started writing well. If you have the basics, you'll be okay. A lot of good writing is common sense.

I'm not going to pound you to pieces with grammar. I'm going to lead you gently through correcting the biggest mistakes I see regularly and explain why these are very bad mistakes. I'm also going to help you with a bit of "re-education," to help clean up a lot of junk you may have learned along the way.

Then, as you go along in your life and career, you can look up questions you have online or in books to clarify a point. There's a lot that I haven't covered in this book. But that's not the point of my effort here. My point is to get you working in the right direction, and then leave the rest up to your own ability.

If you have forgotten your basic grammar (and many have), there's a section in this book that will refresh you.

You acquired this book because you want to be better in some way, and I respect that. So I'm not going to beat you up. I'm going to help you.

Alex Eckelberry

# The English Language.

English is, in my opinion, a great language. And understanding where it came from can be helpful. So enjoy this brief and simple history lesson. It's not vital, so you can skip it. But you might find it useful (and even interesting).

**How it all started**
Many thousands of years ago, there were tribes of people in a large area east of Turkey. These tribes all spoke a very similar language.

These tribes moved to or invaded places to the east and to the west. To the east, they went into Persia (modern-day Iran) and India, and their language became the basis of the Iranian and Indian languages.

In the west, their language became the basis of almost all of the European languages we speak today. Because it went to Europe and as far east as India, this original language is called "Indo-European" (there's a map at the end of this book if you're curious to know more).

You can still see Indo-European in many basic words, such "mother, "father," "brother." These words are similar in all major European, Indian and Iranian languages because they share the same roots.

Pretty interesting, eh?

Now, we move up in time and come to English.

**English is a German language**
Many people don't realize that English is actually related to *German*. It's a *Germanic* language.

Two thousand years ago, the Romans conquered the island of Britain and took over. They prospered as Romans for about 400 years until the Roman Empire started collapsing.

The fall of the Roman Empire was not a pretty time. Soon, the people of Britain found themselves surrounded by a lot of Germans who had moved into the island (often peacefully, sometimes not so peacefully). These Germans came from northern Germany, and were mostly members of tribes, called the Angles, the Saxons and the Jutes.

Over time, these German tribes established seven kingdoms in the area known today as England, which is the southern part of the island of Britain (the northern part being Scotland, and the major western parts being Wales and Cornwall).

The language of the German tribes became Old English, and you wouldn't understand it if it was heard today. It's an old form of German.

Now, prior to invading England, these German tribes had picked up Latin words from Romans over hundreds of years of interaction with the Roman Empire. So it may surprise you to learn that many of the Latin words in English are not necessarily from when the *Romans* conquered England. They were often part of the *German* language of the tribes that came to England.

These seven German kingdoms lived relatively peacefully, until getting into all sorts of nasty fights with invading Vikings from Denmark, who conquered and started putting Danish words into our language; and then several hundred years later another unfortunate thing happened when a region of France invaded England.

So now the poor Englanders were ruled by French-speaking people, and French became the language of the upper classes in England.

Finally, England threw the bums out after all sorts of nasty conflicts, but now the language had words from French, Danish, and, because England was a Christian country, from the Latin used in church (called Ecclesiastical Latin, which means "church Latin"). And, because England was a trading nation, we continued to pick up words from other cultures, even Arabic (such as "orange" and "scarlet," both of which come from Arabic).

Then things got even more interesting when England started conquering other countries and words were brought in from wherever the English happened to go.

So it's a pretty rich language! Interestingly, there are many words in English that have almost the same meaning but have a different "feel," depending on their source. Words from German feel more "earthy" and "real." Words from Latin feel more sophisticated. For example, "go" is from German, while "depart" is from Latin. Both mean almost the same thing, but they *feel* different.

**The grammar police**

Now, about 400 years ago, the grammar police got involved. They wanted to make rules for this language because it was so non-standard. However, they did something that confused things quite a bit: Because they knew Latin (the language that all well-educated people knew), they put Latin rules of grammar into the language.

In Roman times, the common people spoke Vulgar Latin (vulgar here means "common," *not* "nasty") and the well-educated spoke Classical Latin.

Classical comes from a word meaning "the highest rank," and Classical Latin was *very* complicated and definitely the "highest rank" of Latin. The belief at the time was that learning it taught rich young Roman boys how to think. It was *really* hard.

The normal people didn't care, as they just went on their happy way and spoke Vulgar Latin. You could, however, immediately tell who was a member of the upper class when they spoke: their speech was a grammatically perfect form of Latin that was very different from Vulgar Latin.

Well, the grammar police forced rules from this complex Classical Latin into English. There is a major problem with this idea. Latin is Latin – a dead language. It's not English, which is a constantly changing language with a different structure.

Forcing Latin rules into English has made grammar incredibly confusing. English is not Latin: it's a mixed-up Germanic language – like a mutt dog – that has bits and pieces of many different cultures in it.

## Why you still need to understand some grammar

English grammar may sometimes be silly and poorly understood by most. But at least having an understanding of the basics is important. Remember what I said earlier about playing a sport and breaking the rules: you will irritate others. Grammar establishes the basic rules of good speaking and writing, and just like anything with rules, you need to follow them.

However, hopefully I've made you feel a little better about having some difficulty with grammar. It's really not your fault.

# (Almost) Everything you need to know about grammar.

The following is very basic information. But even though it may be taught in school, it's not well understood by many. So here is a quick look at the basic parts of grammar.

You can skip it if you know your grammar well. You can also skip it if you just don't care to read it.

### Words are like Lego blocks of the language

Words are incredibly cool. The English language is like a giant Lego® set, where you get to choose what parts you want to use to create the effect you want.

Let's imagine we are back in time, when cavemen were trying to communicate. For example, they wanted to tell each other about someone (*Caveman John*), what he did (*hit*), and to what or whom his action was directed (*lion*).

> *The caveman hit the lion.*

That is a complete, grammatically perfect sentence.

But it's boring, so the cavemen added a bit more. They added a word to show where the lion was hit (*on*), and added more about where the action was directed (*head*).

*The caveman hit the lion on the head.*

And now that is a perfect sentence, with more added to it.

What if the caveman said this, instead?

*On lion caveman head hit on.*

It wouldn't make much sense, would it?

Who said grammar should be confusing? It's not. You use grammar right now, without even thinking about it.

## Confusions

Words can sound alike but have different meanings. This can make the language confusing. For example, "they're" sounds like "there." These confusions are a source of a lot of mistakes.

Words can also be used together to mean something completely different than what you would expect. For example, "give it a shot" means to "try." These are called *idioms* and are a source of vast confusion for people, especially foreigners.

*How* words are used is called the *parts of speech*. A word can change from one part of speech to another just by the way it's used in the sentence. For example, in "you *run* to the store" and "he had a good *run*," "run" is being used in two different ways, even though it's the same word.

So, now let's look at the parts of speech.

## Words are used to name things. These are called nouns

"Noun" comes from a Latin word meaning "name." Nouns name people, places or things.

*fish, house, man, New York.*

If you're naming something specific, you capitalize it.

*Tom, Paris, Germany*

If it's not specific, you do <u>not</u> capitalize it:

*man, city, country*

(Incorrectly capitalizing nouns is a common and very ugly error.)

Nouns can name one thing (singular) or name many things (plural).

*boy* (singular), *boys* (plural)

**Words can take the place of nouns. These are pronouns**
Pronoun comes a Latin word meaning "in place of a noun."

Pronouns take the place of a noun (words like *I, he, him, her, they,* or *that*).

You know all the pronouns. You use them all the time. It's the word taking the place of a noun in a sentence.

If you didn't have pronouns, writing would look awkward:

Alex likes cars that Alex can drive fast.

instead of

Alex likes cars that *he* can drive fast.

Different pronouns are used in different situations. Not understanding the pronoun and its different uses is the cause of most major grammar errors. I'll get into that a bit later.

**Words can show action or existence. These are verbs**
Verb comes from a Latin word meaning "to speak." Verbs show action.

*swim, love, run*

Verbs can also show how something or someone is *existing*. These are called *be* verbs because they are all different forms of the word *be* (*be, is, were, am, are, was*).

> "Hey, how *are* you?"
> "I *am* okay."
> "Oh good, I was worried that you *were* not okay."

Verbs can be used to show that something is happening in the past or present. This is called *tense*, from a Latin word meaning "time."

> He *runs* (present).
> He *ran* (past).

To show the future, you add another verb that shows something will happen in the future. Joining two words together creates a *compound*, which means two or more things combined. So we call it a *compound verb*:

> He *will run* (future).
> I *am going* to be a rock star (future).

The way a verb changes when it is used in different ways is called *conjugation*.

**Words can give more information. These are adjectives and adverbs**

In grammar, "modify" means to give more information about something. Adjectives and adverbs are modifiers – words such as "beautiful," "ugly," "fast" or "faster," used to give more information about another word.

An adjective modifies a noun. An adverb modifies a verb or another adjective, and often ends with "ly."

*Beautiful* woman (adjective).
*Really* beautiful woman (adverb).
She runs *fast* (adverb).

Adjective comes from a Latin word meaning "added to a noun"; adverb comes from a Latin word meaning "added to a verb."

Simple.

## Prepositions show relationships

Prepositions are often misunderstood, but they are *very* simple.

Prepositions show relationship between other words in the sentence. By "relationship" is meant how other words in the sentence are connected to each other.

Is the cup *under* the table, *over* the table, or *beside* the table?

Do you see the idea of relationship there? The cup is *related* (connected) to the table by being *under* it, *over* it, or *beside* it.

Preposition means "positioned before" because often (but not always), they are placed before the word to which they are showing the relationship.

Words like *on, over, under, beside, above,* and *with* are all prepositions.

(Yes, it really is that simple.)

## Conjunctions join

Conjunction comes from a Latin word meaning "joining together."

Conjunctions join words or groups of words.

If we didn't have conjunctions, writing would look very awkward.

Bill Tom went to the mall.

Tom went to the mall bought an Xbox.

Heather liked the boat not the car.

Here are the same sentences, with conjunctions:

Bill *and* Tom went to the mall.

Tom went to the mall *and* bought an Xbox.

Heather liked the boat, *but* not the car.

There are different types of conjunctions, such as: *and, also, either, or, neither, though, yet, but, however, for, that, because, since, therefore, then, if,* and *unless.*

## Articles

The word *article* sounds like something incredibly complicated. But articles are really easy.

*Articles* are used to communicate whether you're referring to a *specific* thing or a *general* thing.

If it's a specific thing, it's called a *definite article.* If it's not specific, it's an *indefinite article.*

*A* boy (indefinite article).

*An* astronaut (indefinite article).

*The* boy (definite article).

There are only three articles in the entire language: *a, an,* or *the.*

*An* is generally used before words starting with *a, e, i, o* and *u. A* is used before words starting with every other letter.

## Interjection

The final part of speech is the *interjection,* which comes from a Latin word meaning "placed between." It's a word (or words) placed in your writing to show emotion. An exclamation mark often follows an interjection, but not always.

*Ouch!* That hurt!

*Whoa!* Where did you get that hat?

*Oh no.* I forgot my homework.

So, the parts of speech are:

- Noun
- Pronoun
- Verb
- Adjective
- Adverb
- Preposition
- Conjunction
- Article
- Interjection

And that's all you have to know for now about the parts of speech.

**Possession**

In grammar, there is the idea of "possession" (ownership), and it's often misunderstood and leads to major mistakes.

Possession can be actual possession, or the *idea* of possession.

> *Bob's* car

Bob owns – *possesses* – the car.

> The *house's* lights were bright.

The house has lights, but it's more like the *idea* of possession.

Some more examples:

> *His* bicycle. *Her* car. *Their* house.

There are two ways to show possession: using a pronoun that shows possession (such as *his, her, their, your, its*); or by using an apostrophe ('). I will explain apostrophes later in this book.

Not understanding possession is the cause of *many* embarrassing writing mistakes.

Right now, I just want you to get the idea of possession. Later, I'll discuss in more detail how to avoid these mistakes.

**The subject: who or what is "verbing"**
The *subject* is who or what is doing the action in a sentence. This is a very, very simple concept.

Keep it simple.

> *Bill* went to the mall.

Bill is the subject. *Went* is the verb.

Since verbs can also show state of existence (the *be* verbs), you can also have a subject look like this:

> *Bill* is happy.

Bill is the subject. The verb? *is*.

More examples:

> *He* had a great time.
> *She* had a better time.
> *They* had a fantastic time.

*He, she* and *they* are all subjects in these sentences.

Not understanding what a subject is also causes people to make mistakes. More on that later.

**What is d*oing* the action and what is *getting* the action**
This section might be a bit difficult for some. If you can't get it, don't

worry, as I will give you simple rules later to avoid mistakes. However, it's worth understanding, so try to follow along with me.

When a noun or pronoun does the action, it's called the *subject*. When it's *receiving* action, it's called the *object*.

> Bill hit *Tom*.

Tom is receiving the action of being hit by Bill. Tom is the object (poor Tom).

Now, certain pronouns are used when *receiving* action (*her, him, it, me, them, us,* and *you*). These are called *object pronouns*.

Certain pronouns are used when *doing* action (*he, I, it, she, they, we,* and *you*). These are called *subject pronouns*.

Not understanding this fact will cause you to make silly mistakes. However, you don't have to learn complicated grammar rules to figure this out. It's common sense.

Look at this sentence:

> Bill hit *he*.

That looks totally wrong, doesn't it? You're using the wrong pronoun. Instead, it should be:

> Bill hit *him*.

Another mistake:

> John loves *I*.

"I" is used for subjects, like "I love John." It is never used as an object.

To make the sentence correct, you would use an object pronoun:

> John loves *me*.

Other examples:

> Bill loved *her.*
> Bill hated *them.*

Not understanding where the action is directed explains why people make this common mistake:

> She and *him* went to the mall.

The wrong pronoun, *him,* is being used. She and this guy, together, are actually the subject, simply joined by a conjunction.

*Him* is only used for showing who is *receiving* an action.

It should be:

> She and *he* went to the mall.

If you understand the idea of the "object" in grammar, you will avoid many mistakes.

But again, if you don't care or can't understand this concept, I have some tricks later on that will help you.

This is a basic overview of grammar and will give you a foundation on which to build more knowledge in your own time. It is not complete, but to add more would make this book overly complicated.

Then, no one would read the book, or use the information in it.

# (No, I don't really hate fish.)

**Sentence**

A sentence is a single complete thought.

> I hate fish.

The single complete thought is "I hate fish."

Now, we'll make it a bigger sentence:

> I hate fish because I break out in a rash.

Still a single thought. Still a sentence. You're just explaining it a bit more.

You don't do this:

> I hate fish because I break out in a rash and all sorts of terrible things happen because I really hate eating fish and did I tell you about the time I ate a fish and it really turned out badly?

That's called a run-on sentence and it is terrible. Write your thoughts one at a time, each in their own sentence.

A sentence usually has at least two things: something spoken about and something said about it.

John ran.

*John* is being spoken about and *ran* is what is being said about John.

However, there is such a thing as a one-word sentence, usually used in fiction or casual writing:

Do you like cats? *Yes!*
He hit the ball. *Hard.*
*Home.* That's how Kansas felt to her.

## Let's talk about paragraphs

A paragraph is a bigger thought than a sentence but is all one thought.

"I hate fish because I break out in a rash when I eat it. One time, I was in Hawaii and ate a fish, and I had to run to the pharmacy to get medication. Let me tell you: I hate fish!"

This is a complete thought on the subject of "disliking fish." It's a bigger thought that just "I hate fish." But it's all the same idea, and that's a *paragraph*. It's all the same big thought.

Let me show you how it *wouldn't* be done:

"I hate fish because I break out in a rash when I eat it. One time I was in Hawaii, and ate a fish, and I had to run to the pharmacy to get medication. Let me tell you: I hate fish! One day I was wearing pants and didn't like the color. So I decided it had something to do with my dislike of fish. I started only buying pants that were not anywhere near the color of a fish, but then I came to realize, fish come in every color imaginable. So now I don't wear pants!"

Look at what happened: the reader is completely confused, with two different big thoughts joined together. First, it's about hating fish, and then, there's this whole separate idea about pants.

If I had just split the ideas out into two paragraphs, it would have made sense.

I recommend keeping your paragraphs short. Long paragraphs are boring and difficult to follow. Ideally, keep your sentences short as well.

**Put a space between your paragraphs**
This seems like something very simple, but in emails, I often see paragraphs written without any spaces between them. Just press the big Enter key on your keyboard to make one, nice, fat space between the paragraphs.

**Clauses (stay with me here)**
You can skip this part, but you might find it helpful.

Simple sentences are good, but sometimes they can be a bit boring. So, we might want to make them more interesting by adding more.

To do this, we join groups of words that are each "mini-sentences," into one sentence to make a more complex, richer thought.

*Each of these groups of words is called a clause.* Clause comes from a Latin word meaning "a brief statement."

Clauses are a source of considerable confusion for people, and that's not their fault. It's been made very confusing.

I'm going to try and make it very simple: There are two main types of clauses – those which express their own complete thought, and those which rely on another clause.

Clauses that express their own complete thought are called *independent clauses*. Clauses which rely on another clause are called *dependent clauses*.

Let's start with a simple sentence:

> I love cats.

That is a complete thought, but you want to say a bit more. So you add "because they are so cuddly."

> I love cats *because they are so cuddly.*

"Because they are so cuddly" depends on the other clause. It can't stand on its own. It's a *dependent* clause.

Let's go back to a simple sentence:

> I love bicycles.

In this case, you want to add that you *dislike* motorcycles. So you add "I dislike motorcycles":

> I love bicycles, *but I dislike motorcycles.*

These are two independent thoughts, each *independent* clauses. They can stand on their own. To make the writing understandable, they are joined by a conjunction, a word that joins clauses (the word *but*).

That's it. End of lesson. If you want to study more about clauses, get a good grammar book. But I do not want to kill you with this information. I want you to live.

# General writing tips.

Good writing is:

- Pure
- Clear
- Precise

*Pure* means that the writing is in *just* correct English, without anything else added.

Pure writing doesn't include:

- foreign language words
- unnecessary technical words
- old, unused words
- slang

*Clear* means writing that uses normal, simple words and does everything possible to avoid confusion. Words are not used that might be misunderstood to mean something else. Clear writing also does not show off or use complicated terms that no one understands.

*Precise* means writing that intends to have the reader completely understand what is being communicated with as few words as possible.

Precise writing has the goal of getting something understood immediately understood by the reader. It is writing that doesn't use long, boring sentences. It doesn't overuse words. However, it is not so short as to be baffling.

## The best writers

The best writers have something they want to say, and they want the reader to actually get it.

It is not a sign of intelligence to use big words and long sentences. Sometimes, it's a sign of being a jerk.

There is a word to describe someone who shows off, is dull and highly academic: *Pedant.*

That's probably the most complicated word in this book. I only mention it so that you know how to call someone who writes like they have mothballs stuck in their mind, who writes to show off and who is incredibly wordy to the point of being totally uninteresting.

Just because someone uses big words does not mean they are smart.

Don't worry about looking dumb by writing simply. Great writers write simply.

I have a large vocabulary – larger than most people. But I go out of my way to choose simpler words in my writing.

Paula LaRocque, a teacher who wrote a well-known (and excellent) book on writing, used to have her students write as much as they could in 10 minutes. Just… go!

Because of the time pressure, she found that the writers all used simple words. But what surprised her even more was that the writing was excellent!

It was only when the students tried to "write well" that their writing became boring and dense.

Interesting.

*Also, realize people are not as educated as they once were.* It's important to understand that no matter how smart *you* are, the majority of the population is actually very poorly educated. And I include some college-educated people in this statement as well. I remember being in a college writing course where I was surprised at the lack of education of fellow students.

If you're involved in any form of teaching, you will agree: what was acceptable in the past as an elementary school education is now taught in college. If you don't believe me, search online for "8th-grade tests from the 1800s." The level of education of even poor country kids was better than what "smart" city kids get these days.

You will lose any reader if you try to get fancy.

Don't write to seem smart. Write to get your point across. Generally, a good rule is to keep your words at the vocabulary level of a 15-year-old and you'll be safe.

Write to be understood. Write with simple words.

**Get your words right**

There is a bizarre idea in education that one "figures out the meaning of a word by its context." There are many smart teachers who give this terrible advice.

This thinking leads to major errors.

Look at the following sentence:

He was so *noisome*. We hated him being around us.

What do you think the word "noisome" means? Looking at the context and thinking about it a bit, you might think that "noisome" means "noisy."

So then you decide to sound cool, and you write something like this:

The neighbors were upset because I was *noisome*.

You just got trapped by the "figure the word out by its context." You just wrote that you smell terrible. Noisome means *smelly*!

These kinds of mistakes happen quite often.

## Do a lot with a little

A good writer packs a punch, writing with as few words as possible, to get the most information to the reader in the shortest sentence possible.

Look at the difference in these two sentences:

She was so incredibly stunning, so beautiful and wonderful to look at that all men were crazy about her and would constantly bother her. When she would go out, men were constantly asking for her number and she would just ignore them.

Here is the same idea, but shorter, with more punch:

Her beauty drove men crazy. When she went out, men would ask for her number, only to be ignored.

Look at this boring sentence:

Bill went scuba diving in Aruba last January, but he wasn't able to see all the sights that he wanted to, so instead he went back in March to dive more to see what he had missed, and was able to complete all of his diving satisfactorily.

Grammatically, it's fine. But what a completely boring sentence! I can't teach this because it's common sense. When you write something, look to how you can remove anything that's not necessary. It's a discipline that is learned.

Here's the same sentence, re-written:

> Bill went scuba diving in Aruba last January but missed some areas, so he went back in March and completed all of his dives.

## Start with the main idea first

Generally, write your sentences starting with the main idea. Then add more information to your first sentence.

> France in the summer is a beautiful place to visit. The countryside is beautiful, with rolling hills, pleasant fields, lazy rivers and carefree living. Best of all, you'll enjoy incredible food and wine, as you journey through a country that values quality of life over anything else.

There is another style of writing, where you *end* with the main idea:

> A beautiful countryside with rolling hills, pleasant fields, lazy rivers and carefree living, where one enjoys incredible food and wine while journeying through a country that values quality of life over anything else. France in the summer is a beautiful place to visit.

Do you see the difference? The first example is simply easier to follow. The second style is fine, but better used in creative or informal writing. In normal everyday writing, it's hard to follow

## A tip to give your writing laser focus

Ask yourself this question when starting out a writing assignment.

1.  What is the piece of writing about?

2. What is this piece of writing *really* about?

Example:

1. This book is about how to become a better writer.
2. This book is about how to avoid common mistakes in everyday writing so you can be successful .

The first question is weak and general. The second question gets down to specifics. It's a useful tool that you can try yourself[1].

**Use subheads**

Subheads – the boldface introductions to paragraphs like you see in this book – are used because they work. In a fast-paced world, readers skim rapidly through most writing, scanning the subheads. Make them informative on their own, so the reader can quickly pick up what's being discussed just from the subhead.

**Writing longer pieces**

Thinking logically is key in all writing.

It starts with a sentence, itself a complete thought. Sentences are put into paragraphs, which are themselves bigger thoughts. Then a longer piece of writing, such as an essay, is one really big thought.

A common practice for longer pieces is to state the overall idea that you're going to discuss in the first paragraph, and then expand on it as you go further down. It's tidy and neat. Logical. You don't ramble on and on, putting in "oh, and there's this other thing I meant to say" halfway through the document. It shows a scattered, disorganized mind.

---

[1] Thanks to Ann Gynn at the Content Marketing Institute for this great tip.

A similar and often-used writing style is called the "inverted pyramid." This style is where you get all the key pieces of information in the first paragraph, and then the less important points further down. This is the style used by reporters and is useful in writing things like newspaper articles.

**Vary your sentence length.**
Don't let all of your sentences be the same length. A good sentence length is 15-20 words long. However, you should use both longer sentences and shorter sentences to create a rhythm in your writing.

**Sentence fragments**
This part sounds complicated, but it's common sense.

> Research show that children do better learning music at a young age. For example a 15% increase in IQ.

Look at that last sentence. It's a fragment – something just sitting there, not joined to anything. It's confusing.

Instead, just restructure your sentence to make it clearer:

> Research shows that children do better in life when they learn music at a young age. For example, one study showed a 15% increase in IQ for children who studied music at a young age versus those who studied no music at all.

**Babbling**
One error I see quite a lot is weird sentences that just kind of babble, just using a comma:

> She is really nice, she is always doing good things for the poor.
> He wrote the book, he found himself wildly successful.

What's happening is that there are two "mini-sentences" making up the sentence (these "mini-sentences" are called independent clauses).

When you're joining parts of a sentence like this, use words such as: *and, but, for, yet, nor, so, after, although, before, unless, as, because, even though, if, since, until, when, while, however, moreover, on the other hand, nevertheless, instead, also, therefore, consequently, otherwise,* and *as a result.*

> She is really nice, and as a result, is always doing good things for the poor.

> He wrote the book, and consequently, found himself wildly successful.

You can also use a semi-colon (;), which is really a way to join two sentences; it's very useful.

**Get active**

Verbs have "voice," a fancy word that means that the verb shows whether the subject is giving or receiving action.

Active voice verbs show *giving* action, passive voice verbs show *receiving* action.

*Active*

> Tom *hit* the ball
> *She kicked* the wall
> The car *damaged* the bike.

*Passive*

> The ball *was hit.*
> The wall *was kicked.*
> The bike *was damaged.*

You don't even need to know grammar to understand passive versus active voice. You can "feel" it in the writing. Get the idea of something *doing* something, and you've understood active voice.

You can easily change a sentence to active voice:

> *Passive*
> The book *was written* by Mary Jones.

> *Active*
> Mary Jones *wrote* the book.

Active words make the writing come alive. It's a secret to powerful writing. Marketers use it to sell. And you can use it to make your writing livelier and clearer.

Now, some people love to use passive voice to disguise something that's their fault:

> "The bridge was blown up," said the general.

No one is taking responsibility for the bridge being blown up – especially that general. (You can, of course, use this trick yourself!)

## Prepositions

Don't overuse prepositions. In fact, try to keep them to a minimum. You can sometimes remove them completely.

Look at the following sentence:

> The car was driving *at* an incredibly fast pace.

Well, just get rid of the preposition and tighten up the sentence:

> The car was driving incredibly fast.

## Use bullet points

Bullet points are a valuable tool to create effective, clear writing.

Look at this paragraph:

> It's simple to have satisfied customers. You only need to create a great product, deliver great service, communicate regularly, and ask customers for advice on how to improve.

It's not a very easy sentence to read. So, you could use bullet points to make it clearer.

It's simple to have satisfied customers. You only need to:

- create a great product,
- deliver great service,
- communicate regularly and
- ask for advice on how to improve.

Here are some pointers to keep in mind when writing bullet points:

- Keep them simple and uncluttered. Don't use sub-bullet points and sub-categories.
- Keep them each roughly the same length as the rest, so that they are neat and orderly.
- Start them each with the same part of speech. Don't, for example, start one with a verb and then use a noun to start the next one.

Also, good bullet points don't each need to be a complete sentence, but they should be consistent with each other. In other words, make each bullet point a complete sentence, or make each one an incomplete sentence – but at least make them all the same way.

There is a matter of style when it comes to bullet points, so not everything has to be perfect. Just look at the bullet points to see if they are neat, uncluttered and logical.

**Give it a night. And read it aloud.**
If you're not under a deadline, a good idea is put aside what you've written, and read it with fresh eyes the next day. Another tip is one that many professional business writers do: they read the text aloud

to themselves. It's often amazing how a mistake will pop-out when text is read aloud, which is never caught when reading silently.

## How to write

Years ago, when I was first starting in my career, I had a writing assignment from my boss. I was embarrassed to ask "what do I write?" His answer? Just *start* and write what you would normally say to someone.

It's good advice. Just *start*. Write as if you're talking to the person being written to, and the words will start to flow. Then, go back and polish things up to make it all look good.

The key is start writing. By writing, you develop your style. And write *a lot.*

Joseph Devlin, who wrote a masterpiece in 1910 on writing, has some wonderful words on the subject of writing. Take them to heart (I've edited them a bit for modern language):

*"The best way to learn to write is to sit down and write, just as the best way how to learn to ride a bicycle is to ride it. Write first about common things, subjects that are familiar to you.*

*Never hunt for subjects, there are thousands around you. Describe what you saw yesterday— a fire, a horse, a dog-fight on the street. Imitate the best writers in their style, but not in their exact words. Know what you write about, write about what you know.*

*To know you must study. The world is an open book...nature is one great book, the pages of which are open to anyone.*

*Don't think that a college education is necessary to succeed as a writer. Far from it. Some of college men are dead-heads, useless to the world and to themselves. A man may know so much of everything that he knows little of anything.*

*If you are poor, that is not a bad thing but an advantage. Poverty is an incentive, not a drawback. Better to be born with a good, working brain in your head than with a silver spoon in your mouth.*

*Employers are constantly on the lookout for good talkers, those who are able to attract the public and convince others by the force of their language.*

*It is possible for everyone to become a correct speaker if he persists and take a little care.*

*Listen to the best speakers and note carefully the words which impress you most."*

---

There's a bit of an art to writing well. It comes from reading a lot and from practicing a lot. You'll develop your style over time, but remember to keep the basics in there.

Practice good writing and it will help you in life. It will help you in telling stories and facts, and to think more logically.

# That's it. Period.

Punctuation.

It comes from a Latin word meaning "inserting pauses in writing."

Get that? *Pauses.*

Periods. Commas.

*Pauses.*

There is a tale about a wonderful writer, James Thurber, when asked about his use of a comma:

> "Why did you have a comma in the sentence, 'After dinner, the men went into the living-room'?"

> "This particular comma," Thurber explained, "was a way of giving the men time to push back their chairs and stand up."

(This story comes from a great book about punctuation, *Eats, Shoots & Leaves.*)

Punctuation has now come to mean all the little symbols we use to make text understandable and, sometimes, more interesting.

## Period
A period (.) ends a sentence.

## Comma
A comma (,) creates a pause in the text. There is more to the use of a comma, but if you keep to this simple definition for now, it will get you a long way (just don't go crazy and overuse them).

## Exclamation mark
An exclamation mark (!) shows strong emotion or shouting, but don't overuse it. Use it only when you *really* need to!

## Question mark
A question mark (?) turns a sentence into a question.

## Colon
A colon (:) is used to list out a number of things in a sentence.

> Three people came to the party: Bill, Tony, and Sue.

It can also be used to give more information, as long as the part after the colon can act as a sentence on its own:

> I'm looking for a copy of this book: one of my friends wants to read it.

You can also use colons to greet someone in a formal business letter:

> Dear Mr. Roberts:

(Never use a semicolon in this situation. For informal letters, use a comma instead of a colon.)

You do not need to capitalize the word that comes after the colon, unless it would normally be capitalized. (There are times when you would capitalize the first word, but generally, you'll be totally fine if you don't.)

## Semicolon

A semicolon (;) makes two sentences into one; I use this one a lot. Two separate thoughts mashed into one! Yummy!

## Ellipses

Ellipses comes from a Latin word meaning "to leave out," and shows that some text has been removed.

> "Bob ate the whole sandwich" can be changed to "Bob ate the...sandwich."

Ellipses are also handy to just... create a pause... in the text...as if words are going unspoken. (This use is frowned upon by grammar police, and you shouldn't overuse it, but it can create a nice effect in your writing when used carefully.)

Ellipses are always three periods. It is such a common error for writers to use five periods, or two, or six, that if I had a dime for every time I spotted it, I'd be really rich. Unfortunately, I won't get rich this way (and doing a cheap book isn't going to help, either).

## Parentheses

Parentheses come from a Latin word meaning "putting beside," and are the symbols ( ). They are used to give a bit more information about something, or to make a remark about something. They are a useful tool that can be used to create a nice effect in your writing, or to clarify something.

> Bill made it to the meeting on time *(this was a first)*.

> Joanie *(who had hit her head earlier that evening)* did not appear happy at the party.

There are some minor errors you can make with parentheses that are not worth discussing here. Keep in mind, however, that sometimes a comma can be used instead of parentheses, and that choice is yours. And, like everything in writing, don't overuse parentheses.

Now, if a sentence is on its own, in parentheses, the period goes *inside* the parentheses.

> Joanie laughed out loud. *(She rarely laughed.)*

Otherwise, the period goes *outside* the parenthesis.

> Joanie laughed out loud *(she rarely laughed)*.

Notice that a different feeling and idea can be communicated by how you write. Both of the above examples are acceptable English; they are simply different ways to communicate the same thing.

## Quotation marks

Quotation marks (" ") are used primarily to show that someone is speaking.

> "Hello," said Gary, "how are you?"

You also use quotation marks to show that a word is not part of the rest of the sentence:

> The word "love" comes from German.

Use quotes (or *italics*) for titles of books, magazines, new technical words, special or unusual words, and so on:

> The book "Call of the Wild" is one of the great American novels.
> This was a method of torture known as *enhanced interrogation*.

If a quote is inside a quote, use a single quotation mark:

> "He told me 'the British are coming' and I laughed," said Tom.

Punctuation marks go inside the quotes:

"What's up, Joanie?" asked Tom.

"Nothing important," said Joanie.

I spent my spare time reading "Oil Drilling News."

(This is the American English way of doing it; it's done differently in Britain, where you put the punctuation marks outside of the quotes.)

**Dashes and hyphens**

A hyphen is different than a dash. A hyphen is short. A dash is longer. Each do different things.

- A hyphen is the "-" key on your keyboard.

Use a hyphen to create compound words, joining two words to make a new one:

> *off-campus*
> *Janet Hall-Wilkinson*
> *merry-go-round*

Use a hyphen for numbers that do not show a range of numbers (a range of numbers would be something like "1 through 10," which I discuss further below). Keep your hyphens to things like phone and social security numbers:

> 111-55-1111
> 800-555-1212

Use a hyphenated word to make things clearer to the reader. Look at this sentence:

> He filled out the stolen vehicle form.

It's confusing. You would use a hyphen to make it clearer:

> He filled out the *stolen-vehicle* form.

What you're actually doing in this case is using a hyphen to create an adjective from two words.

Here is another example:

He lived in a *well-planned* community.

(Never use a hyphen when one of the words ends with "-ly.")

It's not a crime to create words with hyphens that are new to people:

He worked with *computer-generated* art.

Interestingly, many hyphenated words become, themselves, single words:

*Wet-suit* became *wetsuit.*
*Black-bird* became *blackbird.*

As a last note, hyphens never have spaces on either side.

– An en-dash is a bit longer than a hyphen (it's called "en" because it is about the same size as the letter "n" in older printing machines).

En-dash means "through." So you would use it for ranges of things:

July–August
pages 12–15

— An em-dash is used to replace a comma or parentheses (it's called "em" because it is about the same size of the letter "m" in older printing machines).

Using em dashes makes for a lively, fast-paced kind of writing.

He went to the store – the big store in the mall – to get what he wanted.

I don't think it particularly matters if you have a space before or after en and em dashes. I think it's a matter of style. Hyphens, however, never have spaces.

Most word processors will automatically create an em dash when you type a word, a space, two hyphens, another space and then a word. For en dashes, type a word, space, hyphen, space, word.

Alex Eckelberry

# The misunderstood apostrophe

I've dedicated a short chapter to the *apostrophe*, since it is the most misunderstood punctuation mark of all.

The apostrophe is the ' sign in a word. It means something (a letter or letters) has been *removed*.

That's *all* it means.

If you get one thing out of this book, it's to understand how an apostrophe is supposed to work!

Apostrophes are used in two different ways: To show a word has been created from two words (contraction) and to show possession.

*Contraction*
In English, we contract (join) words to be a little lazy. "We are" becomes "we're." The apostrophe shows that the letter "a" has been removed.

But it's confusing, because contracted words sound the same as other words.

> *We're* sounds the same as *were* or *where*.
> *It's* sounds the same as *its*.

49

*They're* sounds the same as *their*.
*You're* sounds the same as *your*.

You will need to know the differences so that you too don't make these common mistakes.

*Possession*
An apostrophe is also used to show possession (ownership). As I discussed earlier in this book, possession a very interesting concept in grammar. You can make it clear that someone or something "possesses" something. Get the concept of "possession" and you'll really get this one. It's not always *literally* possessing something. It's more of an *idea* of possession.

However, even in possession, *the apostrophe is still removing a letter*, and this fact is not understood by most people. Listen up: you will soon be smarter than about 95% of your friends.

In older English, the way you showed possession was to add "es" to a word. For example, there's a book by a fellow named Henry Chaucer, written 700 years ago. Here is something he wrote:

Christes gospel

He showed that it was the gospel of Christ by adding "es."

Later, people just took out the "e" but showed it had been removed by using an apostrophe.

Christ's gospel.

Neater, tidier, quicker, cleaner.

Here is another example of the idea of possession, using an apostrophe:

This is the house that Jim owns.
This is *Jim's* house.

We know Jim possesses (owns) it.

Or:

> The house had bright lights.
> The *house's* bright lights.

The house doesn't actually "possess" bright lights, but it's the *idea* of possession.

There are a few simple rules for apostrophes used in possession:

For a noun showing one thing (singular), add *'s* at the end.

> The *horse's* hair.
> *Tom's* shirt.

For a plural noun already ending in "s," simply add an apostrophe at the end.

> *Guys'* night out.

*Plurals*
A common mistake is to use an apostrophe to make something plural (more than one).

For example:

> The two *boy's* went to the store.

This is a mistake. Remember, an apostrophe means a letter has been *removed*. It should be:

> The two boys went to the store.

Here are some examples of the correct use of apostrophes with plurals. We'll start with the simple example of a horse.

> A *horse* – a single horse.
> Two *horses* – more than one horse

Then, a single horse, showing possession:

A *horse's* tail – the tail of a horse.

But what if we want to describe several horses possessing something? In older English, we would have added "-es" at the end:

The horseses tails.

But that's older English and honestly, it looks ridiculous! Because we're hip and modern, we use an apostrophe to remove the whole "-es" at the end.

*The horses'* tails – the tails of the horses.

These are the important rules for apostrophes. There are more rules which you can look up online if you like.

# Common mistakes: Don't do this at home. Or anywhere.

Here I've listed the major mistakes made in today's writing. I've ignored quite a few errors, focusing primarily on the common ones.

**The biggest mistakes**

*It's* = it is. "It's a cold day."
*Its* = a pronoun. "I hate the sound of *its* motor."

*We're* = we are. "We're sitting here."
*Were* = a verb. "What were you doing?"
*Where* = a pronoun. "Where are you?"

*They're* = they are. "They're coming to dinner."
*Their* = a pronoun. "Their car broke down."
*There* = a pronoun. "I went there and it's beautiful."

*You're* = you are. "You're beautiful."
*Your* = a pronoun. "Your car is nice."

**There vs. their vs. they're**
This error is probably the most common one in writing and is a source of enormous irritation to some people.

These words sound alike, so it's understandable if they get confused. But to be totally honest, if you misuse these words, you will really, really irritate a large group of people.

Here's the scoop:

*There* means a *location*.

> I went *there*.

*Their* means a group of people.

> *Their* car broke down.

*They're* means "they are."

> *They're* more people than expected.

**I or me?**
(I covered this problem earlier in this book and am going to go over it again a bit, but if you really don't care, just scan down to the section named "A trick.")

*Me* is used when *me* is receiving something.

You use pronouns like *me, him, her, it, us* and *them* when the pronoun is the *object* (again, "object" means that the pronoun is receiving something).

As an example, look how weird these sentences look:

> He hit *he*.
> I went with *they*.
> Come with *we*.
> Bring it to *I*.

These sentences look wrong because you're using pronouns that are used as *subjects* (what is being talked about). Instead, you should be using pronouns that are used as objects. The sentences should be:

He hit *him*.
I went with *them*.
Come with *us*.
Bring it to *me*.

That's why some people cringe when you say something like this:

Jim and *me* went to the beach.

"Jim and me" is being used as the subject (even though there's two people – Jim and me, they are both being used as <u>one</u> subject). *Me* is never used as a subject. It should be *I*.

Jim and *I* went to the beach.

*A trick*
People can get confused when you have two people being talked about in the sentence.

However, there is a trick if you can't remember what to do or if you simply don't care about rules.

If you can't figure out if it's *me* or *I*, take out the <u>other</u> person.

Look at this example:

Jim and *me* went to the beach.

Take out "John" and you'll see that "I" is correct:

__ __ I went to the meeting.

(It's obvious that "me" is incorrect.)

The same rule works with myself, and the other "selfs." See the next section.

**The selfies**
It's very simple to understand when to correctly use *myself, himself, yourself, itself* and *themselves*: The subject (what's being talked about

in the sentence) has to be receiving the action from the object (the "self").

It's called a "reflexive pronoun" because it "reflects" back on the subject.

People often make the mistake of just using "myself" without understanding what it means. *It means that you did something back to yourself.*

Sound confusing? It's really not.

> I hit myself.

In this case, "I" (the subject) received the action from "myself" (the object).

Some other examples:

> He hit himself.
> They hit themselves.
> You hit yourself?
> It broke itself.

You don't say things like:

> The doctor talked to myself.
> The teacher and myself talked.
> Myself will be with you in a minute.

It can be confusing if you're dealing with two people, such as:

> Jim and myself went to the party.

Incorrect. It should be:

> Jim and I went to the party.

If you're confused, use the same rule used to figure out whether to use "me" or "I": Take out the other person and it will make sense what word to use.

> _____ and myself went to the party.

Obviously wrong.

> _____and I went to the party.

Correct.

## Does "I" come first or last?

This upsets people with a strong feeling of self-importance, but in grammar, <u>you</u> come last when talking about yourself.

Not:

> _Me_, Mary and Joseph went to the beach.

Instead:

> Mary, Joseph and _I_ went to the beach.

You're last.

I know, sucks, huh?

## Starting a sentence with but, or, and

Old-school English teachers do not like children to start their sentences with the conjunctions _and, but, or, nor, for, so_ or _yet._

This is more of an effort to ensure good writing habits than from any really good reason. Professional writers have been using conjunctions to start sentences for a long, long time.

For formal writing, I would not start a sentence with a conjunction. However, for more informal, casual writing (including even most business writing), who cares. I don't.

**Match up your nouns and pronouns neat and tidy**

I've discussed this before in this book, and I can show you the grammatical rules, but it's really common sense.

Take a look at this sentence:

> John's ideas inevitably led *him* into a conflict between *he* and his boss.

The sentence talked about John's ideas leading *him* into a conflict, and suddenly it's *he* and his boss?

Instead:

> John's ideas inevitably led *him* into a conflict between *him* and his boss.

Or this:

> Because *the farmers* were the ones who believed in less taxes, no other groups but *them* were at the meeting.

It was *the farmers* who believed in less taxes, and then *them* went to the meeting? No, wrong.

Instead:

> Because *the farmers* were the ones who believed in less taxes, no other groups but *they* were at the meeting.

**Incorrect placement of modifiers**

Look at the following sentence:

> Oozing slowly across the floor, Marvin watched the salad dressing[2].

---

[2] Thanks to the Writing Center at the University of Wisconsin – Madison for this brilliant example.

It seems like Marvin is oozing slowly across the floor. It's a *terrible* sentence structure.

The fix is simple: Put your modifiers *next* to the words they are modifying.

> Marvin watched the salad dressing *oozing slowly* across the floor.

Or, even better: Use common sense. This sentence would never have been written if the writer just looked at the sentence for what it was: crazy!

## Confusing pronoun use

Have you ever looked at a sentence and wondered just what the heck the sentence meant? Sometimes, this problem is caused by pronouns used confusingly.

For example:

> Bob was really smart, always fixing cars and radios, and *this* was how he was able to get through college so rapidly.

What is "this" referring to? Is it referring to his being "really smart," or to his ability to fix cars and radios?

An English teacher once taught me to always place what is being referred to after the "this." So the sentence would read:

> Bob was really smart, always fixing cars and radios, and *this intelligence* was how he was able to get through college so rapidly.

You can do that. But really, it's just a matter of how you construct the sentence. You could, for example, rewrite it:

Bob was always fixing cars and radios as a kid, and this intelligence was how he was able to get through college so rapidly.

Just check to make sure that pronouns clearly point to what is being written.

## Parallelism

Parallelism is a fancy word that means that the verbs that you use are all of the same type in a sentence.

Look at the following sentence:

Learn to *run* faster, and *eating* better foods.

*Run* is a verb, and so is *eating*. *Instead,* use *run* and *eat.*

Learn to *run* faster, and *eat* better foods.

It sounds like a no-brainer, but this mistake is not uncommon.

## Commas

Commas put a natural pause into a sentence. There are rules around commas, but I don't want to confuse you too much. Just look at it logically.

Here's an example:

Joe ran to the bank went to the store and came back an hour later.

Yikes. I am out of breath just reading that sentence!

Instead, just a simple comma makes everything work beautifully:

Joe ran to the bank, went to the store and came back an hour later.

Use commas when inserting a bit of additional information:

> Bill, always unhappy, was really upset that Janet came home late.

Use commas in a series of things:

> Bill, Tom, Janet, and Bob all went to the store.

Use commas before words like *and, but, for, nor, yet, or, so* when joining groups of words.

> It was a wonderful day outside, and we played the whole time.

If you could put the word *and* in a series of adjectives, then a comma usually belongs there:

> A fine handsome blond man came to the house.

Or

> A fine *and* handsome *and* blond man came to the house.

Or, correctly:

> A fine, handsome, blond man came to the house.

Overusing commas is also a mistake. It makes the sentence hard to read and understand:

> He went to school and took, in several weeks, courses such as, English and History.

Instead:

> He went to school and took, in several weeks, courses such as English and History.

Another way you can overuse a comma is being lazy and not separating out one sentence into two sentences. This is a very common error:

> By the middle of the twentieth century and after two major wars, the Germans had finally found a way to become citizens of the world without conflict, instead using their power as an economy to gain the dominance in the world that they so desired.

This sentence is endless! I'm lost and confused and tired reading it.

Let's make it clear and simple, by separating it out into separate thoughts:

> By the middle of the twentieth century and after two major wars, the Germans had finally found a way to become citizens of the world without conflict. Instead, they used their power as an economy to gain the dominance in the world that they so desired.

As I've said before, you can also use semi-colons as a nice way to combine two sentences into one.

These are the major rules on commas; when you're up to it, there are good references online that have additional rules.

**Wrong placement of the space at the end of a sentence.**
Does this not look wrong to you? It should.

> He is great !
> I like books .

This error is very common in online writing (especially with older people). I don't really understand why, but some people write the word, then press "space," and then put in the punctuation mark.

Obviously, the punctuation mark goes at the end of the sentence, with no space between the final word and the punctuation mark.

**Don't double up your punctuation**

He is great.!
What was the reason.?
That was such a great movie!!!

Keep to one punctuation mark. Only one!

He is great!
What was the reason?
That was such a great movie!

## Who or Whom

The misuse of who is a personal peeve of mine. But it's now such a common error in language that I'm not sure it even matters.

Nevertheless, if you want to sound like a smarty pants, get it right. Well-educated people really do notice the correct use of "whom."

The grammar rules are actually simple: "whom" is a pronoun which receives action (the object) but it might get confusing.

So here is a simpler trick: "He" is the same, grammatically, as "who." "Him" is the same, grammatically, as "whom."

You hit him.
You hit *whom?*

He is nice.
*Who* is nice?

She drove him.
She drove *whom?*

It was addressed to him.
To *whom* should I address it?

So you can just replace who or whom with "he" or "him" and see what sounds right.

Alex Eckelberry

# Using the right word.

Here are some examples of mistakes where the wrong word has been chosen.

**Infamous, famous, notorious**
These three words are commonly confused.

*Famous* is what you read about on TMZ (celebrities, that sort of thing). Or something widely known to be fabulous.

> That Hollywood actor is *famous*.
> Her cooking was *famous* throughout the neighborhood.

*Infamous* means the complete opposite – something terrible and horrible!

> He was an *infamous* serial-killer.
> Her temper was *infamous*.

*Notorious* also means famous, but usually for a bad reason.

> *Notorious* Wall Street bankers.

**imply vs. infer**
These words are actually opposite in meaning and are commonly confused.

To imply means to hint at something. To infer means to make an educated guess.

> Jon *implied* that Bill had an odor problem.
> By John's comment, I *inferred* that Bill had an odor problem.

## Then is not than

*Then* is a point in time. *Than* shows comparison.

> Back *then*, I would have rather eaten candy *than* have gone to school.

## You're welcome. Not "your welcome"

*Your* is a pronoun. *You're* means "you are."

## Ensure vs. insure

Ensure makes something certain.

> Using this wonderful book will *ensure* I'll write well.

Insure? That's Obamacare. Car insurance. Getting insurance for a business.

> How can you *insure* him? He has a DUI!

The words are not the same.

## I better go

"I had better go" or "I'd better go." Not "I better go."

## Definately?

Do you not use a spell-checker? Because if you are, it's *definitely* not working.

## All together, altogether

*All together* means "all in one place." *Altogether* means "completely."

The family came *all together*, which was *altogether* a wonderful thing.

## Discrete vs. discreet

*Discreet* means being careful not to attract attention or reveal a secret. *Discrete* means separate.

I *discreetly* asked if she was single.
There are two *discrete* buildings on the lot.

## Along or a long

*Along* means going with someone or something, or forward motion. A *long* means great length.

We drove *along* the beach for *a long* time.
My sister went *along* with me to the movies, and it was *a long* wait in line.

## Advice vs. advise

You give *advice*. You *advise* someone.

## Nauseated vs. nauseous

*Nauseated* means you're sick.

I felt *nauseated* after a bad dinner.

*Nauseous* is something that makes you feel sick.

The smell was *nauseous*.

## Misspelling won't

*Won't*, meaning "will not," is never *wont*. There is always an apostrophe.

He *won't* (will not) go to the store.

(You might be interested to know that "won't" is a contraction of "wonnot," an old English word with the same meaning.)

There is a different and rare word, "wont," without the apostrophe. But it means *someone's typical behavior:*

> He is *wont* to hate disco.

(Meaning his normal behavior is to hate disco.)

**A lot is *two* words**
Not *alot*.

A lot.

**At least is two words**
Not *atleast*.

At least.

**To is not too**
*Too* means "also," or "excessively." It doesn't mean the same thing as "to."

> *To* eat candy is *too* dangerous.

**Tho vs. though**
I had a business partner who would use "tho" in writing constantly, and although he was very well educated, it truly made him look illiterate.

There is no such word as *tho*. Use *though*.

**Accept and Except**
You *accept* something, *except* something that you don't want.

**Capital or Capitol**
*Capital* is money for a business, or the city where the government of a region or a country is located.

*Capitol* is a building where lawmakers meet. It's a hard one to remember, but try.

## Emigrate or immigrate

*Emigrate* is to <u>leave</u> a country. *Immigrate* is to <u>enter</u> one.

## Toward and anyway never have an "s"

You go *toward* something, not *towards*.

Oh, and "anyways" is not a word. It's just *anyway*.

## Dollar symbol

Some people have a confusion with how to write currency – specifically the US dollar.

The dollar sign comes before, never after.

> Incorrect: 2$
> Correct: $2

It's different for other countries, however. Check your local currency.

## For all intents and purposes

For all intents and purposes mean "practically speaking."

> For *all intents and purposes*, he was done with college, as he had finished his final exam.

Not "for all intensive purposes."

## Farther vs. further

A lot of people have difficulty with this one, but the rule is simple. These words both basically mean the same thing, but one is used for physical distance, while the other is used for an *idea* of distance.

Use *farther* when talking about physical distance (like feet or miles).

> How much *farther* is it to the store?
> If I walk any *farther*, I'm going to faint.

Use *further* when it's an *idea* that's like distance, but isn't actually a real distance.

> I went *further* in my career than the others.
> Would you like any *further* information?
> No *further* questions were allowed.

In truth, no one will kill you over this one. The words have been used interchangeably for hundreds of years.

## Formerly vs. formally

Formerly means previously, or before. Formally means very proper and serious.

> She was *formerly* the wife of the senator.
> He spoke very *formally*, choosing his words carefully and acting very serious.

## Precede vs. proceed

Precede means to go before. Proceed means to go forward.

> The groom always *precedes* the bride in a wedding.
> Please *proceed* down the aisle.

## Affect and effect

Affect means to do something that causes an effect.

> "It *affected* our profit," not "it *effected* our profit."

There is another use of the word "effect," meaning to do something: "To effect change." But it's still not "affect."

## Principle and principal

*Principal* is a key thing, or a person who runs a school. *Principle* is something you believe in.

## Lend vs. borrow

You *borrow* something *from* someone. You *lend* something *to* someone.

## Numbers

There are differences of opinion, but I spell out the number if it's under 10, and just write the number if it's 10 or over.

> I ate three pieces of chicken, and then ate another 10.

There are more rules for numbers that can be found online. But my little rule is widely accepted.

## "Could care less" is simply wrong

You could care less? That actually means you *could care less*. It's nonsensical. Instead, it's "couldn't care less."

## Irregardless

This word has become accepted but I wouldn't use it, because it's a dumb, sloppy word.

The *ir-* at the front means "not" and *-less* at the end also means "not." So you've stated the same thing twice.

Like I said, it's a dumb, sloppy word. Just use "regardless."

## Compliment vs. complement

Compliment is a nice thing you say to someone. Complement means something goes well with something.

*Very* common error.

> I *complimented* her on how well the drapes *complemented* the sofa.

*Complimentary* can mean to say something nice, or to give something for free:

Her *complimentary* remarks about the house made Jim feel good.

The drinks were *complimentary*.

## Moot vs. mute

A *moot* point is something that isn't worth discussing. *Mute* is being unable to speak.

## i.e. vs. e.g.

**e.g.** means *for example*. **i.e.** means *specifically*. Misuse of these two is a very, very common mistake.

He ate food (i.e. candy).

He *specifically* ate candy.

He ate food (e.g. chocolate, jelly beans, and so on).

These are examples of what he ate.

He missed his flight (i.e. flight 254).

You're specifically saying what flight he missed.

He missed his flight (e.g. one of the evening flights).

Not specific. You're just giving an example of one of the flights he missed.

## Peek, peak, pique

Pique means to stimulate ("it piqued my interest").

Peak is the top part of something.

Peek is to look in to a place.

It *piqued* my curiosity. He *peeked* into the room. He reached the mountain *peak*.

## Who or That?
"Who" is used in referring to <u>people</u>. "That" is used in referring to <u>things</u>.

> She is the girl *who* came to the office.
> The car is the one *that* hit the curb.

## Adverse or averse
*Adverse* is something harmful. *Averse* means not liking.

> I was *averse* to eating food with *adverse* effects.

## Setup or Set Up?
You *set up* something. It is then *setup*.

## Into or In to?
Use into only if it shows *movement*.

> He went *into* the room.
> He called *in to* the meeting.

## That or which?
You can drive yourself crazy with this one, and the truth is, no one really cares much these days if you use "which" or "that." I also don't want to kill you with the grammatical rules.

However, it's very important for lawyers, as they need to make things very clear. So lawyers, pay attention.

To the rest of you, read this if you want to be a really careful (and good) writer. Then, you'll know when to use "which" or "that."

"That" is used when what is being discussed is clearly part of the sentence. It's not separated by a comma, because it's key.

"Which" shows you that it's not as important to the meaning of the sentence. It might be important, but it's not key to getting the sentence.

> The ball *that* was in the room was round.
> The ball, *which* was in the room, was round.

Do you see the subtle difference? In the first sentence, it's a ball *that was in the room*. It's specific. (People! It's the ball that was in the room! Hello! Is this mic on? It's the ball that was in the room!)

In the second sentence, we just note, as part of the conversation, that this was the ball in the room to make things clearer.

Also, "which" always has a comma before it, and "that" doesn't.

## & or and?
Use "and," not "&." Never, ever, ever use "&" in formal writing. Save "&" for naming products or companies.

## Should have vs. should of
There is no correct usage for "should of." None.

## Moreover vs. more over.
It's moreover.

## Peruse
Peruse means to study something very carefully, *not* to skim through.

## Loath or loathe
A very common mistake is to confuse these two words.

*Loath* means unwilling, *loathe* means you dislike.

> I was *loath* to go to the park, because I *loathe* the filthy pigeons.

## Elicit or Illicit
You *elicit* (bring out) something. If you're doing something *illicit*, well, you're doing something very bad, because it means "illegal."

## Allusion and Illusion
You allude to something (talk about it indirectly). That is an *allusion*.

An *illusion* is what you see from a magician – that kind of thing. The words are not the same.

## Penultimate does not mean "the best"

*Penultimate* means before the last thing:

> The *penultimate* show in the TV series.

Here, penultimate means there is *one more* show left.

It does not mean "the best." Very common error.

## Fewer vs. less

Fewer is used for plural. Less is for singular.

> *Fewer* horses are on the farm.
> *Fewer* than 80 kids showed up to the party.

> Spend *less* time in traffic.
> *Less* than $10 in his pocket.

## Recur or reoccur

Something *recurring* happens again and again and again.

> A *recurring* role on television.

Something *reoccurring* happens again, but not necessarily again and again and again.

> The area suffers from *reoccurring* tornadoes.

There are more mistakes, but these are the major ones.

Alex Eckelberry

# Advanced Class.

Here are common mistakes that are a little more advanced. If you've managed to get through this book and are still alive, read on.

**Between you and me**
Confusion about which pronoun to use when using the word "between" is common.

First, it's never "between you and I." It's "between you and me."

Here's why: when a pronoun is receiving something, it's an *object pronoun*. Object pronouns include *her, him, it, me, them, us,* and *you.*

The "between" in the sentence is a preposition, and "me" is the object of the preposition.

The easiest trick is just to take out the other party to see if it sounds right. "Between ____ I" or "Between _____ me," well, "me" is clearly the winner.

**Lay and lie**
(This section is not about the word "lie," as in "to tell something that's not true," which is rarely a source of mistakes.)

The best writers get the difference between "lay" and "lie" wrong all the time. It's really hard to remember the rules.

However, I have, perhaps, a really simple way to look at it: Lie and lay have different meanings.

*Lie* means to recline ("lie down").

*Lay* means to put down ("lay your pen on the paper").

If you understand these two meanings, it will make things simpler.

If you're going to "lay your daughter down," you're going to *put her down*. You wouldn't "lie her down."

It gets confusing when you're talking about the past, though.

Here's a simple table. It's not complete, but covers most of the mistakes you can make:

|  | *Present* | *Past* | *Completed in the past* |
|---|---|---|---|
| **LIE** | *I **lie** down* | *I **lay** down* | *I had **lain** down* |
| **LAY** | *I **lay** the pen on the paper.* | *I **laid** the pen on the paper* | *I had **laid** the pen on the paper.* |

Try your best. No one will kill you if you don't get it right. You can always check online for the correct use.

**Ending sentences with a preposition**

Prepositions – words that show relationship (such as *at, in, on, below, under, above, over, about*) aren't supposed to be at the end of a sentence. However, this rule has been broken so much, no one cares, and the reason behind the rule is idiotic anyway.

There's an old joke my brother Stephen loves to tell about ending a sentence with a preposition:

A Texas boy walks into Harvard and asks a student for directions to the bathroom.

"Hey, buddy, where's the bathroom at?" asks the Texan.

"Sir, we at Harvard do not end our sentences with prepositions," the Harvard student responds, with a superior look.

"Okay, where's the bathroom at, jerk?" says the Texan.

The whole "ending sentences with a proposition is evil" came out of trying to make Latin rules work in English. Preposition, in Latin, means "put before," and in Latin, a proposition is always placed *before* what the preposition is relating to.

Well, in case you haven't noticed, English isn't Latin. So, it's not something to fuss *over*. Or worry *about*.

## Agreement

This section also may be a bit difficult. However, if you want to write well, you should try to understand it.

Words must all line up and "agree" with each other.

This means that the correct verbs and pronouns are used if there is a singular or plural subject.

This sounds complicated, but it's not. It's common sense and if you speak English well, you already have all of your words in agreement.

The key to understanding agreement is whether or not the subject of the sentence is singular or plural.

Singular is *one* thing.

A *boy*.

Plural is more than one thing.

Two *boys*.

Verbs and pronouns are used differently if the subject is singular or plural.

Look at how the verb changes if the subject is singular or plural:

A boy *is* eating ice cream.
Two boys *are* eating ice cream.

Pronouns change based on singular or plural:

The girl left *her* purse inside.
The girls left *their* purses inside.

The key is to remember that if it's a plural, plural verbs and plural pronouns are used. If it's singular, singular verbs and singular pronouns are used.

You have to think a bit sometimes to write this correctly.

For example:

*One* of the cars *are* open.

This is incorrect. *One* is the subject, not *cars*. We're talking about *one* of the cars. The subject is singular, so, you would use a singular verb:

*One* of the cars *is* open.

Another example:

He *don't* like it.

*Don't* is actually *do not*. Would you actually say "he do not like it"? Of course not. Instead, you would use the verb used for singular subject, *does*:

He *does not* (*doesn't*) like it.

Another example:

Either *are* correct.

Either (*one* thing) is singular. So the sentence is incorrect. It should be:

Either *is* correct.

You have to get the idea of singular and plural for this all to make sense. For example, words like *the news* is singular, because we think of it as one thing.

The news *is* on at 6 pm.

I'm not going to list out all the verbs and pronouns for you, or give you a big list of rules (you can look these up online if you like). Common sense will get you very far.

**Split infinitives**
You have to be a grammar dork to care about this issue, and I certainly don't.

An infinitive is a verb which has the word "to" in front of it.

*To serve* you is our goal.

You're not supposed to split the infinitive – meaning – don't put a word in between "to" and the verb:

*To* better *serve* you is our goal.

Instead, it is supposed to be:

*To serve* you better is our goal.

However, you'll find examples of split infinitives regularly used in the English language these days, and it's not a big deal. I'm careful with it, but I also realize that following this rule sometimes makes my writing less interesting.

I wouldn't worry about it.

**English is a Subject Verb Object language**
As a final note, it might be helpful for some to understand that
English is a language in which sentences have a pattern:

> Subject Verb Object

In other words:

> Tom hit Bill.

So, it's called a Subject Verb Object language (or, SVO).

This is useful to know only because some foreign language students
have a really hard time with English. I've done a lot of one-on-one
tutoring work with foreign language students, and have experienced
their confusions first hand. They come from countries which have a
different pattern.

German, for example, is a Subject Object Verb (SOV) language:

> Tom Bill hit.

Realizing that there many languages have different patterns may help
you if you're an ESL student, or if you're teaching ESL.

There are plenty of references on the net with regard to SVO, SOV,
and other patterns that are not worth getting into in this simple book.

# Business letters.

Most dictionaries include information on writing business letters. There are also plenty of references online. However, below is a brief overview.

**The simple business letter**
The easiest type of business letter is all lined up on the left.

Start with your name and address.

Below that, the date.

Below that, the address of the person you're writing to.

Then, the greeting (called the "salutation"):

Then, the text of the letter.

Then, the closing ("Sincerely," "Yours truly," etc.)

And finally, your name.

It should look something like this example when you're done:

---

John Doe
Account Manager
Industrial Sales, Inc.
23 Doe Street
Boston, MA 02108

March 28, 2015

John Roberts
Purchasing Manager
Acme Supplies
55 Park Avenue
New York, NY 10012

Dear John,

It was a pleasure meeting you on Friday about our new industrial samples. I have included our latest brochure for your review.

I look forward to continuing our discussion.

Sincerely,

John Doe
Account Manager

---

(Of course, if you have a corporate letterhead, you would not write your address on the top, as it would already be written on the letterhead.)

Salutations can have a colon after them, or just a comma.

> Dear Mr. Roberts:
> Dear Mr. Roberts,

If you are writing to a woman whom you know is married, use *Mrs.* If you're writing to a woman whose marriage status is unknown, use *Ms.*

> Dear Mrs. Roberts,
> Dear Ms. Blakemore,

These days, it's usually acceptable to use the first name in a business correspondence with someone you are already in communication with (especially in America).

> Dear John,
> Dear Janet,

However, you would not address a person in a position of authority using their first name, unless it was an informal letter. The decision to use the first name or last name comes down to common sense and judgement.

If it's a formal letter where you don't know the name of the recipient, you can use any of the following:

> Dear Sir or Madam:
> To whom it may concern:
> Dear Hiring Manager,

If you're writing someone in a position of authority (congressman, mayor, judge, royalty, etc.), search online for the correct salutation. There are too many different rules to include in this simple book.

There are different closings you can use:

Yours truly,
Sincerely,
Sincerely yours,
Respectfully,
Regards,

It would be incorrect to capitalize both words in the closing:

Yours Truly,

Only the <u>first</u> word is capitalized.

Your truly,

However, keep it simple. It's fine to just close with "Sincerely." You don't need to get fancy.

**Business emails**
Just because you're using email doesn't mean all the rules of proper behavior go out the window.

Some pointers:

Make sure *your* name (in the FROM field) is professional.

Not "j doe," but "John Doe."

Make sure the recipient's email address is professionally written (in the TO field).

Not "j roberts," but John Roberts.

If you don't know the person, address it formally.

Dear Mr. Roberts,

If you have already spoken to the person, you can be more informal.

John,

Don't use fancy formatting. Stay away from colors. Stay away from different types of fonts. No pictures of unicorns, rainbows or any other such silliness. Keep it very, very clean.

Write normal, full sentences. Just because it's an email does not mean it's a free-for-all in casualness.

Your closing is just like a business letter.

Sincerely,

For informal communications, skip the closing. Just write your name.

Keep your signature simple. No pictures of your kids, flowers, huge and unnecessary graphics and other clutter. Remember that graphics often just become attachments, so use them carefully – if at all.

Of course, your LinkedIn information and typical business contact info is totally fine and expected.

John Doe
Industrial Sales, Inc.
23 Doe Street
Boston, MA 02108
Phone: 617-555-1212
email: Jdoe@industrialsalesinc.com
www.industrialsalesinc.com
(Don't use http:// in your website.)

The website www.businessemailetiquette.com has some useful additional pointers.

# And now, for the even more adventurous

I wrote this book because something has been nagging at me for years: the often bad use of English online, in social media (Facebook, etc.) and emails. So, I decided to write a simple book to help others.

People who make grammatical mistakes often have no idea why they make mistakes, and may bristle at correction.

I'm not interested in "correcting" people. I'm interested in helping people write better, so that they can become a more integral part of the community.

This book was written to help the majority, and there is much more that I could add (and might in subsequent editions). However, I've purposely kept the text of this little book very simple. I've even put the credits in the back, as opposed to footnoting throughout the text (very distracting).

However, for the more adventurous, I've opened up a bit here and discuss some of what I've written about in this text. I'm also breaking my earlier rule of only talking at the level of a 15-year old.

**Grammar**
I was fortunate, many years ago, to read a book called *The New*

*Grammar*, by L. Ron Hubbard. This book is a little-known but fascinating discussion of the subject of grammar, and includes a new and sensible grammar for the English language.

The book (and its companion, *Small Common Words Defined*) also has all sorts of additional tidbits that I drew upon in this book, such as the re-inclusion of the article as a part of speech (lost in many grammars); the Indo-European roots of the language; the fact that grammar describes what has happened in language, as opposed to creating rules for what *should* be (the "descriptive" vs. "prescriptive" approach); and the imitative development of language (called "onomatopoeia").

Much of my inspiration and general ideas about grammar I credit from Hubbard's work. While better known for founding a religion, his studies on teaching, grammar and education have spawned a movement; and an organization, Applied Scholastics, has been created to promote his educational philosophy through a non-religious approach. I highly recommend picking up a copy of The New Grammar for any unanswered questions. It's the best (and simplest) grammar book I've found.

**Grammar Police**

My mention of Latin grammarians shoehorning English into Latin rules is not just idle talk. The Oxford Words blog refers to this group as "Latin-obsessed 17th century introverts"[3].

And, from the dreaded Wikipedia:

> "The first English grammar, *Pamphlet for Grammar* by William Bullokar, written with the seeming goal of demonstrating that English was quite as rule-bound as

---

[3] "Grammar Myths #1:…" OxfordWords Blog. Web. 28 Nov. 2014. blog.oxforddictionaries.com/2011/11/grammar-myths-prepositions

Latin, was published in 1586. Bullokar's grammar was faithfully modeled on William Lily's Latin grammar, *Rudimenta Grammatices* (1534). Lily's grammar was being used in schools in England at that time, having been "prescribed" for them in 1542 by Henry VIII. Although Bullokar wrote his grammar in English and used a "reformed spelling system" of his own invention, many English grammars, for much of the century after Bullokar's effort, were to be written in Latin; this was especially so for books whose authors were aiming to be scholarly. Christopher Cooper's *Grammatica Linguæ Anglicanæ* (1685) was the last English grammar written in Latin.

The yoke of Latin grammar writing bore down oppressively on much of the early history of English grammars. Any attempt by one author to assert an independent grammatical rule for English was quickly followed by equal avowals by others of truth of the corresponding Latin-based equivalent. Even as late as the early 19th century, Lindley Murray, the author of one of the most widely used grammars of the day, was having to cite "grammatical authorities" to bolster the claim that grammatical cases in English are different from those in Ancient Greek or Latin."[4]

Rational linguists view language through *use* (descriptive). A rules-based method (prescriptive) method of viewing the language is bound to fail. English is an open language with a potpourri of influences, and it will continue to evolve.

The reality is that grammar is descriptive, not prescriptive, no matter how much grammarians want to fight against an evolving language.

---

[4] *History of English grammars.* (n.d.). Retrieved April 8, 2015, from http://en.wikipedia.org/wiki/History_of_English_grammars

To wit, the French have the Académie française, a national body given the task of keeping the French language pure. In its effort to force continued purity on the language, some asinine decisions have been made – as my friend David Newberger points out – few more infamous than banning the use of the word "computer," instead forcing the French to use "ordinateur," which is a big desktop calculator.

I don't mean to imply that rules aren't needed; there would be no way of learning the correct, current use of the language (and this is especially important in teaching English to foreign language students). There have to be rules, but there must also be a recognition of the natural evolution of the language. As Adrian Williams points out:

> "If we look at history, the English language has transformed from a language that demonstrated 'grammatical gender' to a language that demonstrates 'natural gender'. In Old English, gender was normally marked on all parts of language including noun, adjective, demonstrative and pronoun. But the gender attached to a noun was quite randomly assigned which resulted to a language system of grammatical gender that really had no methodical relationship between biological gender and the gender that marked a linguistic object. In the Old English, the word 'hand' was assigned a male gender while 'pride' was given a female gender and the word 'body' was given a neutral gender. As the English language evolved in due course, genders were no longer used to mark nouns, with some prominent exceptions like the use of 'man' and '-ess' in words that refer to specific professions (milkman, fireman

for both men and women, actress for a female actor and waitress for a female waiter)."[5]

To quote linguist Jean Aitchieson:

> "In brief, the puristic attitude towards language – the idea that there is an absolute standard of correctness that should be maintained – has its origin in a natural nostalgic tendency, supplemented and intensified by social pressures. It is illogical, and impossible to pin down to any firm base. Purists behave as if there was a vintage year when language achieved a measure of excellence which we should all strive to maintain. In fact, there never was such a year. The language of Chaucer's or Shakespeare's time was not better or no worse than that of our own – just different."[6]

The Middle English of Chaucer was just that – the English of Chaucer. It was not better or worse than the English we speak today, although it was vastly different than modern English.

It evolved.

**Indo-European language**
This chart shows the theorized spread of the Indo-European language:

[5] Williams, Adrian J. (2014-03-15). *Linguistics: Language Mastery. The Ultimate Information Book* (Linguistics, Language, Semantics, Syntax, Pragmatics, Etymology, Phonetics) (Kindle Locations 642-647). Jr Kindle Publishing. Kindle Edition.

[6] *Ibid.*

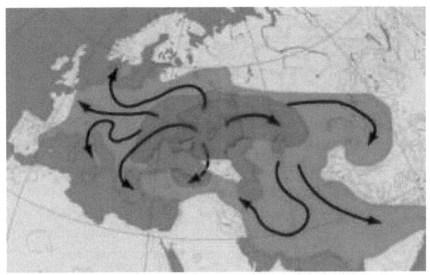

(Credit to Dbachmann)[7]

The theory that all major European and Indo-Iranian languages came from a common ancestor is well established in Linguistics, although the exact nature of the original diaspora continues to researched and debated.

Needless to say, the prevailing thought is that there was an original group of dialects in the region of the Caucuses (modern southeastern Russia, Azerbaijan, Georgia and Armenia) or Anatolia (Turkey), and that several waves of migrations both east and west created the basis of the languages we know today.

To quote William Harris:

> "Most of the ancient and modern languages of Europe belong to a family of languages which is called by modern scholars "Indo-European" and their study falls within the range of research known as Historical Linguistics. It was

---

[7] *Indo-European expansion 4000–1000 BC, according to the Kurgan hypothesis,* Author by Dbachmann, licensed under the Creative Commons Attribution-Share Alike 3.0 Unported license. From Wikipedia, http://en.wikipedia.org/wiki/Indo-European_languages

first noticed by Sir William Jones, a linguistically minded employee of the British East India Company in the late 18th century as he began private lessons in Sanskrit, that most of the languages of Europe bore a strong resemblances to each other in basic, primary vocabulary. These languages furthermore seemed connected structurally with the ancient Sanskrit which he was learning."[8]

I won't exhaust the issue, when frankly, there are better qualified authors easily found through some rapid internet searches.

### The imitative creation of language (onomatopoeia)

The theory of the use onomatopoeia as a developing agent for language is widely discussed in a number of works. The theory's ultimate veracity, however, will probably never be determined, and it continues to be debated among scholars.

It's interesting, for example, to note that *chicken, hen* and *rooster* all have the same onomatopoeic root:

> "An originally onomatopoetic term for 'chicken', 'hen', or 'rooster', derived from *$k^herk^h$-, is attested in a number of Indo-European dialects. Its dialect distribution gives reason to consider it Proto-Indo-European: Skt. *krka-vriku-* 'rooster', Avest. *kahrka-* 'hen', Pehl. *kark* 'hen', *Pers.* kark 'chicken', 'hen', Gk. *kerkos* 'rooster', MIr. *cercc* 'brood hen'; Toch. B *krariko* 'rooster'. In its onomatopoetic character this word can be compared with innovated forms meaning 'rooster' in separate recent branches, based on words meaning `sing', 'cry': Lat. *gallus* 'rooster' (cf. OCS *glastu*

---

[8] Harris, William. "The Indo-European Background." *The Indo-European Background.* Web. 6 Dec. 2014.
http://community.middlebury.edu/~harris/LatinBackground/IndoEuroBackground.html

'voice', Russ. *golos*); Goth. *hana* 'rooster', OHG *hano* 'rooster' (Ger. Hahn), OE *henn* 'hen' (Engl. hen),…"[9]

Darwin also had some thoughts on the subject:

> "The child who was just beginning to speak called a duck 'quack' and by special association it also called water 'quack'. By an appreciation of the resemblance of qualities it next extended the term 'quack' to denote all birds and insects on the one hand and all fluid substances on the other. Lastly, by a still more delicate appreciation of resemblance the child eventually called all coins 'quack' because on the back of a French sou [money] it had once seen the representation of an eagle. Hence to the child the sign 'quack' from having originally had a very specialized meaning became more and more extended in its significance until it now seems to designate such apparently different objects as 'fly', 'wine', and 'coin'."[10]

I leave it up to your own spirit of curiosity to delve into it further. The theory is valid, at least in my view.

## On the "earthiness" of English

English is more visceral, earthy language, a fact pointed out by Henry Hitchings in his delightful book, *The Secret Life of Words*. I quote:

> "Often we have three terms for the same thing – one Anglo-Saxon, one French, and one clearly absorbed from Latin or Greek. The Anglo-Saxon word is typically a neutral one; the

---

[9] Gamqrelize, T'amaz, V. V. Ivanov, and Werner Winter. *Indo-European and the Indo-Europeans: A Reconstruction and Historical Analysis of a Proto-language and a Proto-culture*. Berlin: M. De Gruyter, 1995. Print. Also available on Google Books.

[10] Drummond, Henry. *The Ascent of Man*. Lanham: Start LLC, 2013. Print. Also available on Google Books.

French word connotes sophistication; and the Latin or Greek word, learnt from a written text rather than from human contact, is comparatively abstract and conveys a more scientific notion. Consider, for example, the verbs rise, mount and ascend, or go, depart and exit. In each case, the first word has an Anglo-Saxon source and is informal, the second is French and comparatively formal, while the third is Latin and suggests something more specialized or technical. A more extreme example is fire, flame and conflagration; another, holy, sacred, consecrated."[11]

## On the perceived incorrect usage of "myself," etc.

It's interesting that "incorrect usages" of the "selfies" have been in use by reputable authors for a long time in English. As a reference, I quote this article from Slate Magazine's blog:

"You seem like a better version of myself.

I just want to be myself.

I haven't seen any myself.

I myself haven't seen any.

Myself, I haven't seen any.

You would even say that to me myself?

There are two others here besides myself.

He asked William and myself to do it.

He was a man as big as myself.

Myself, as director here, will cut the ribbon.

---

[11] Hitchings, Henry (2009-09-29). *The Secret Life of Words: How English Became English* (p. 21). Farrar, Straus and Giroux. Kindle Edition.

William and myself will be there.

Myself and William will be there.

I asked myself what I could do.

I directed all inquiries to myself."

The author continues: "…all of the above examples have been in common use in English for as long as there has been an English language (written records go back 1,500 years)… But not all of them are considered acceptable in formal usage by everyone today."[12]

Still, stick with the simple "reflexive" rule. People will get irritated if you use the "self" pronouns incorrectly. And it sounds stuffy anyway, and you don't want to sound pretentious, do you?

## "I'm doing good," "I'm good" and "Think Different"
Get your grammar freak on, because things are going to get a bit hairy here.

What's wrong with this picture?

I am doing good.

Or

I'm good.

A lot of people think the use of the word "good" here is flat-out *wrong*.

Actually, there is nothing wrong, at least grammatically (even though I personally dislike the use of the word "good" used here).

---

[12] Harbeck, J. (n.d.). *Are You Using Myself Correctly? The Fantastic Flexibility of the Reflexive Pronoun.*
http://www.slate.com/blogs/lexicon_valley/2014/01/17/myself_when_is_it_okay_to_use_th e_reflexive_pronoun_in_a_sentence.html

Why do some people get upset? "Good" is an adjective. Adjectives modify *nouns,* not *verbs.*

Here, people will say that "doing" is the verb, and that so you can't use an adjective to modify a verb. Instead, you should use an *adverb* (like "well") to modify a verb.

Except they are a bit wrong.

Good is actually modifying "I," only because there's a *linking verb* there ("am").

Linking verbs do not express action. Instead, they join the *subject* with the *predicate* (the predicate – from Latin, "to assert" – tells us what the subject is or does).

In an odd twist of English grammar, if there is a linking verb between the subject and the modifier, then you use an adjective. It's called a *predicate adjective*[13]. It's an adjective which is predicating (asserting) what the subject does.

This is why English grammar can become so hated.

However, I do think that "well" is a better word choice: "I'm doing well."

You make the decision.

*Think Different*
Now, regarding "Think Different," experts agree that it's obviously supposed to be "Think Differently"[14]. And, I agree. It's just Apple

---

[13] Discussed nicely at *"I'm Good" Outrage Is Nonsense.*
www.motivatedgrammar.wordpress.com/2011/08/03/the-im-good-outrage-is-nonsense/;
and *Good Versus Well.* www.quickanddirtytips.com/education/grammar/good-versus-well.

[14] Olson, L. (2008). *Visual rhetoric: A reader in communication and American culture.* Los Angeles: Sage.

being cute in marketing.

However, there are two arguments that supposedly make it acceptable.

One is that "different" is actually being used as an adverb. I have personally consulted several large dictionaries, and find this argument to be absurd.

There's a different argument, coming directly from Steve Jobs:

> "They debated the grammatical issue: If 'different' was supposed to modify the verb 'think,' it should be an adverb, as in 'think differently.' But Jobs insisted that he wanted 'different' to be used as a noun, as in 'think victory' or 'think beauty.' Also, it echoed colloquial use, as in 'think big.' Jobs later explained, 'We discussed whether it was correct before we ran it. It's grammatical, if you think about what we're trying to say. It's not think the same, it's think different. Think a little different, think a lot different, think different. 'Think differently' wouldn't hit the meaning for me.'" [15]

Hmm...I don't completely buy it. I think they just liked the way it sounded. It certainly sounds more interesting.

And so, with this argument, we come to the close of this book, emphasizing that grammar is not rules-based (prescriptive) but actually descriptive of the changes that occur in language through use.

---

[15] Isaacson, Walter (2011-10-24). *Steve Jobs* (pp. 329-330). Simon & Schuster, Inc. Kindle Edition.

In other words, "Think Different" has now entered the language as acceptable speech, and I'm sure we'll see its use continue in other forms, leading to the simplest possible solution: major dictionaries will add "different" as an adverb.

There's certainly precedent. After all, the entire language has been evolving for the last 1,500 years and will continue to evolve.

In the wonderful movie *Firefly*, we see that English has become a weird mix of Chinese, English and whatever else happened to come along, with odd (sometimes old-fashioned) syntactical rhythms that match the spirit of the space frontier:

```
                Capt. Malcolm Reynolds
   But it ain't all buttons and charts, little albatross. You
   know what the first rule of flying is? Well, I suppose you
      do, since you already know what I'm about to say.

                      River Tam
          I do. But I like to hear you say it.

                Capt. Malcolm Reynolds
   Love. You can learn all the math in the 'Verse, but you take
    a boat in the air that you don't love, she'll shake you off
   just as sure as the turning of the worlds. Love keeps her in
    the air when she oughta fall down, tells you she's hurtin'
            'fore she keens. Makes her a home.

                      River Tam
              Storm's getting worse.

                Capt. Malcolm Reynolds
           We'll pass through it soon enough.
```

And so, as an endnote, whatever storms we will go through in the English language, in the words of Captain Reynolds: "We'll pass through it soon enough."

Good writing.

# Credit where credit is due.

I have avoided using footnotes in this basic book in order to keep the text simple. The various sources I consulted are cited below. Any errors made, of course, are my own.

*General grammar reference:* Hubbard, L. Ron. *The New Grammar.* Los Angeles, CA: Bridge Publications, 1990. Print. http://www.elearnaid.com/newgrammar.html.

Hubbard, L. Ron.. *Small Common Words Defined.* Los Angeles, CA: Bridge Publications, 1990. Print. http://www.elearnaid.com/smalcomworde.html

*General grammar and style:*

Devlin, Joseph. *How to Speak and Write Correctly (1910).* (It is my belief that this book is in the public domain; it can be freely read on Google Books.)

LaRocque, P. *The book on writing: The ultimate guide to writing well.* Oak Park, IL, 2003: Marion Street Press.

*A wonderful book on the subject of grammar and punctuation:* Truss, Lynne. *Eats, Shoots & Leaves: The Zero Tolerance Approach to Punctuation.* New York: Gotham, 2004. Print and online."

*On ending sentences with a preposition and the 17ᵗʰ century introverts:*
*Grammar Myths #1:...* OxfordWords Blog. Web. 28 Nov. 2014.
blog.oxforddictionaries.com/2011/11/grammar-myths-prepositions"

*On the history of English Grammars: History_of_English_grammars.*
Wikipedia. Wikimedia Foundation, Web. 28 Nov. 2014.
http://en.wikipedia.org/wiki/History_of_English_grammars

*Hyphenation*
*Hyphenated Compound Words - When and Why?* (1999, June 1).
http://englishplus.com/news/news0699.htm

And lastly, I am indebted to some wonderful online resources:

The Blue Book of Grammar
http://www.grammarbook.com/

My favorite online etymology site, where I was able to get the
derivations of key words used in grammar so easily:
http://www.etymonline.com/

The delightful Grammar Girl:
http://www.quickanddirtytips.com/grammar-girl

Get it write
http://www.getitwriteonline.com/

The UW–Madison Writing Center
http://www.writing.wisc.edu/

Guide to Grammar and Writing (Capital Community College
Foundation)
http://grammar.ccc.commnet.edu/grammar/index.htm

Ann Gynn, Editor
Content Marketing Institute
http://www.contentmarketinginstitute.com/author/ann-gynn/

A massive list of errors in language, which I found after I'd written the book and wish I'd learned of earlier. Whatever I've missed can be found here.
https://public.wsu.edu/~brians/errors/errors.html

The wonderful Chaucer site at Harvard
http://sites.fas.harvard.edu/~chaucer/

Weber State University, commonly misused words and phrases:
http://wsuonline.weber.edu/wrh/words.htm

Oxford Dictionaries commonly confused words:
http://www.oxforddictionaries.com/words/commonly-confused-words

And more that I can't recall off-hand, but assuredly found their way into my work.

I had many friends online who came up with suggestions as to what they wanted to see covered in this book. Special call out to Sally Berneathy, Sirio Balmelli, John Amussen, JoJo Zawawi, David Newberger and Stephen Eckelberry for their help reviewing this book. To the rest, thank you, I know who you are.

# Index

# About the author

Alex Eckelberry has written and spoken extensively on a broad range of subjects, including technology, the environment and investing. He has nearly 30 years of experience in technology and related areas, including several years in private equity and venture capital. He has been extensively quoted and interviewed in national press, radio and television, including BusinessWeek, The New York Times, USA Today, The Today Show, NPR, Fox News and CBC Canada. His community involvement includes founding the Tampa Bay Conservation League; the Julie Group, which seeks fairness in the intersection of technology and law; and co-founding Phishing Incidence and Response Termination (PIRT). Alex is currently an independent advisor and board member to a broad range of companies, and lives with his wife and four children in the Tampa Bay, Florida area.

# Can I ask a favor?

If you enjoyed this book, found it useful or otherwise then I'd really appreciate it if you would post a short review on Amazon. I do read all the reviews personally so that I can continue to write what people want.

Oh, and if you find something you'd like to see changed in this book, or have a complaint, question or whatever, I'd love to hear from you. Just contact me through my website – www.becomeabetterwriter.org.

Thanks for your support!

Writing Well (for the rest of us)

Alex Eckelberry